Overview of Some Windows and Linux Intrusion Detection Tools

By
Dr. Hidaia Mahmood Alassouli

Evaluation of Some Windows and Linux Security Tools

GFI LANguard, Nessus, Snort, Base, ACID, Rman, SnortCenter, OSSEC, Sguil

1.Abstract:

The paper evaluates some the security tools. Top security tools can be found in http://sectools.org/. Most important vulnerabilities in Windows and Linux can be found in www.sans.org/top20/. The paper covers the installation and configuration of the following security tools:

- LANguard
- Nessus
- Snort
- BASE
- ACID
- Rman
- SnortCenter.
- OSSEC
- Sguil

Keywords: Vulnerability Assessment Tools, Intrusion Detection Tools, LANguard, Nessus, Snort, BASE, Rman, OSSEC, Sguil.

2.What it Does:

In this paper I will evaluate some the security tools. Among my work in this area, I found the best site that lists the security tools is http://sectools.org/. Most important vulnerabilities in Windows and Linux can be found in www.sans.org/top20/. There is a good course that covers most of the hacking and security issues, the Certified Ethical Hacking course.

The paper covers the installation and configuration of the following security tools:
- LANguard
- Nessus
- Snort
- BASE
- Rman
- OSSEC
- Sguil

3.Vulnerability Assessment Tools:

The following vulnerability assessment tools were tested in order to look for the main differences between them when scanning Linux and Windows machine:
LANguard in Microsoft Windows
Nessuss in Windows and Linux

Some other that can be tried also: Tenable NeWT , Shadow Security Scanner, Microsoft Baseline Security Analyzer.

3.1 GFI LANguard:

GFI GuardLAN and Microsoft Base Line Security Scanner are mostly same. Download GFI GuardLAN from http://www.gfi.com/lannetscan/. After installation, you can start scanning any machine with the administrative privilege.

3.2. Nessus:

Download the nessus from http://www.nessus.org and install it.

a) Installation on Windows:
The installation is straight forward. Download the software after registration, and install the package after providing the activation code (you shall get it through email), and the necessary plugins will be downloaded automatically upon the installation. You can use the Nessus Client that installed with the package. You can also create users, download and run NessusWX Client as its output is clearer.

b) Installation on Linux
Installation in Linux needs some preparation.

1- Download the latest version of Nessus from http://www.nessus.org/download/
Install it with the following command depending on your version
      # rpm –ivh Nessus-*.rpm

2- Create a Nessus User. At minimum, one Nessus user should be created so client utilities can log into Nessus to initiate scans and retrieve results.
      # /opt/nessus/sbin/nessus-add-first-user
In the file /opt/nessus/etc/nessus/nessusd.conf there are several options that can be configured. For example, this is where the maximum number of checks and hosts being scanned at one time, the resources you want nessusd to use, and the speed at which data should be read is all specified, as well as many other options.

3- Start the Nessus service as root with the following command:
      # /opt/nessus/sbin/nessusd –D or # /sbin/service nessusd start
      To stop Nessus
      # killall nessusd

4- Depending on your subscription service, you will have received an activation code which entitles you to either the direct feed of plugins or the registered, seven-day delayed feed of plugins. Users who have downloaded Nessus from the regular download page should have received an email containing an activation code for the registered feed. Otherwise, you can go to http://www.nessus.org/register to register your Nessus scanner in order to receive a plugin activation code for the registered feed. To install the activation code, type the following command on the system running Nessus, where <license code> is the registration code that you received:
      # /opt/nessus/bin/nessus-fetch --register <license code>

5- The following command is used to update the Nessus scanner with the most recent plugins:

```
# /opt/nessus/sbin/nessus-update-plugins
```
6- There is a new feature in version 3.0 where Nessus will now fetch the newest plugins on a regular basis automatically. This is done with the auto_update option located in the nessusd.conf file. The default for this option is set to "yes". The option auto_update_delay determines how often Nessus will update its plugins in hours, which has a default value of 24. The plugins update will take place the set number of hours after nessusd is started and will continue every N number of hours after that. For this option to work properly, you have to make sure that the scanner has a plugin feed activation code that is correctly registered. Use the following command to verify this:

```
# /opt/nessus/bin/nessus-fetch --check
```

7- Now the Nessus server is ready to be connected to with a client. There are multiple ways to connect to the Nessus server depending on your type of system. NessusWX is a client available for Windows platforms and NessusClient is an X11/GTK GUI. Command line operation can also be used instead of a client.

8- You can download NessusClient RPM from http://www.nessus.org/download/ and install it. You can run NessusClient by executing

```
# NessusClient
```

9- Users are not required to use a client to connect to the nessusd server and run a scan. They can choose to use command line operation to do this. In order to run a scan using command line operation, you must run the scan in batch mode. To do this, use the following command:

```
# /opt/nessus/bin/nessus –q [-pPS] <host> <port> <user> <password> <targetsfile> <result-file>
```

Where, targetsfile will include the hosts that you would like to scan. The host, port are your Nessus server IP address and port number.

3.3 Testing:

I tried to test the GFI LANguard Scanner on
- Windows machine, providing it the administrator privilege
- Linux machine, providing it the root privilege

I tried to test Nessus on
- Windows machine
- Linux machine

It seems that both tools provides some special type of information, so I don't want to tell which tool is better. I just advice to try both tools when checking the vulnerabilities.

You cant scan the machines behind firewall when using GFI LANguard, but Nessus can do.

4. Intrusion Detection Tools:

In windows I tested the BlackICE for intrusion detection and prventation. I downloaded the evaluation version from www.iss.net/issEn/DLC/blackiceevaluation.jhtml. This tool is good; especially it can detect any newly installed programs or any intrusion in your host. But It cant detect intrusion in the whole network.

For Linux , I saw that Snort is good tool for intrusion detection of the whole network. But snort is not easy tool to configure, so I just looked for some graphical interface for it. Out of my search I found that BASE and the rule manager for snort can be helpful. I will show here step by step guide for installing snort, BASE and the rule manager for snort.

4.1 General Information about Snort:

Snort can be configured to run in three modes:
- Sniffer mode, which simply reads the packets off of the network and displays them for you in a continuous stream on the console (screen).
- Packet Logger mode, which logs the packets to disk.
- Network Intrusion Detection System (NIDS) mode, the most complex and configurable configuration, which allows Snort to analyze network traffic for matches against a user-defined rule set and performs several actions based upon what it sees.
- Inline mode, which obtains packets from iptables instead of from libpcap and then causes iptables to drop or pass packets based on Snort rules that use inline-specific rule types.

If you just want to print out the TCP/IP packet headers to the screen (i.e. sniffermode), try this:
```
# ./snort -v
```

This command will run Snort and just show the IP and TCP/UDP/ICMP headers, nothing else. If you want to see the application data in transit, try the following:
```
# ./snort –vd
```

This instructs Snort to display the packet data as well as the headers. If you want an even more descriptive display, showing the data link layer headers, do this:
```
# ./snort –vde
```

If you want to record the packets to the disk, you need to specify a logging directory and Snort will automatically know to go into packet logger mode:
```
# ./snort -dev -l ./log
```

Of course, this assumes you have a directory named log in the current directory. If you don't, Snort will exit with an error message. When Snort runs in this mode, it collects every packet it sees and places it in a directory hierarchy based upon the IP address of one of the hosts in the datagram.

To enable Network Intrusion Detection System (NIDS) mode so that you don't record every single packet sent down the wire, try this:
```
#./snort -dev -l ./log -h 192.168.1.0/24 -c snort.conf
```
where snort.conf is the name of your rules file. This will apply the rules configured in the snort.conf file to each packet to decide if an action based upon the rule type in the file should be taken. If you don't specify an output directory for the program, it will default to /var/log/snort.

Preprocessors were introduced in version 1.5 of Snort. They allow the functionality of Snort to be extended by allowing users and programmers to drop modular plugins into Snort fairly easily. Preprocessor code is run before the detection engine is called, but after the packet has been decoded. The packet can be modified or analyzed in an out-of-band manner using this mechanism. Preprocessors are loaded and configured using the preprocessor keyword. The format of the preprocessor directive in the Snort rules file is:

> preprocessor <name>: <options>
> preprocessor minfrag: 128

Snort rules are divided into two logical sections, the rule header and the rule options. The rule header contains the rule's action, protocol, source and destination IP addresses and netmasks, and the source and destination ports information. The rule option section contains alert messages and information on which parts of the packet should be inspected to determine if the rule action should be taken.

> alert tcp any any -> 192.168.1.0/24 111 (content:"|00 01 86 a5|"; msg:"mountd access";)

The text up to the first parenthesis is the rule header and the section enclosed in parenthesis contains the rule options. The words before the colons in the rule options section are called option keywords.

The rule header contains the information that defines the who, where, and what of a packet, as well as what to do in the event that a packet with all the attributes indicated in the rule should show up. The first item in a rule is the rule action. The rule action tells Snort what to do when it finds a packet that matches the rule criteria. There are 5 available default actions in Snort, alert, log, pass, activate, and dynamic. In addition, if you are running Snort in inline mode, you have additional options which include drop, reject, and sdrop.

1. alert - generate an alert using the selected alert method, and then log the packet
2. log - log the packet
3. pass - ignore the packet
4. activate - alert and then turn on another dynamic rule
5. dynamic - remain idle until activated by an activate rule , then act as a log rule
6. drop - make iptables drop the packet and log the packet
7. reject - make iptables drop the packet, log it, and then send a TCP reset if the protocol is TCP or an ICMP port unreachable message if the protocol is UDP.
8. sdrop - make iptables drop the packet but does not log it.

4.2 Installing Snort and BASE:

Base is a graphical interface in which you can see all generated alerts generated by Snort IDS.

1- Create the installation directory
```
# cd /root
# mkdir snortinstall
```

2- Download Snort from http://www.snort.org/

3- Download PCRE from http://easynews.dl.sourceforge.net/sourceforge/pcre/pcre-5.0.tar.gz. Install PCRE from source
```
# tar –xvzf pcre-5.0.tar.gz
# cd pcre-5.0
# ./configure
# make
# make install
```

4- Install and set up Snort and the Snort rules:
```
# tar -xvzf snort-*.tar.gz
# cd snort-*
# ./configure --with-mysql
# make
# make install

# groupadd snort
# useradd -g snort snort
# mkdir /etc/snort
#mkdir /etc/snort/rules
# mkdir /var/log/snort
```

From the Snort installation directory /root/snort-*/
```
# cd rules
# cp *  /etc/snort/rules
# cd ../etc
# cp * /etc/snort
```

5- Modify your snort.conf file. The snort.conf file is located in /etc/snort, make the following changes.
```
var HOME_NET 10.12.0.0/16
var EXTERNAL_NET !$HOME_NET
var RULE_PATH /etc/snort/rules"
```

6- Now tell snort to log to MySQL
    output database: log, mysql, user=snort password=password dbname=snort
    host=localhost

7- Download Sourcefire VRT Certified Rules from http://www.snort.org/pub-bin/downloads.cgi. Extract the snortrules-pr-2.4.tar.gz in the /etc/snort/rules directory.

8-Make snort start with the system. Add a line to /etc/rc.local that reads like the following text.
    /usr/local/bin/snort -c /etc/snort/snort.conf -i eth0 -g snort -D

9- Setting up the database in MySQL:
    #mysql
    mysql> SET PASSWORD FOR root@localhost=PASSWORD('');
    mysql> create database snort;
    mysql> grant INSERT,SELECT on root.* to snort@localhost;
    mysql> SET PASSWORD FOR snort@localhost=PASSWORD('password');
    mysql> grant CREATE, INSERT, SELECT, DELETE, UPDATE on snort.* to
    snort@localhost;
    mysql> grant CREATE, INSERT, SELECT, DELETE, UPDATE on snort.* to
    snort;
    mysql> exit

10- Execute the following commands to create the tables
    mysql -u root -p < ~/snort-*/schemas/create_mysql snort
    Enter password: the mysql root password

11- To install BASE, download php-gd package and install it
    # rpm php-gd-*.rpm

12- Download ADODB from
http://easynews.dl.sourceforge.net/sourceforge/adodb/adodb462.tgz

13- Go to download directory and execute
    # cp adodb462.tgz /var/www/html
    # cd /var/www/html
    # tar -xvzf adodb462.tgz
    # rm –rf adodb462.tgz

14- Download BASE from
http://easynews.dl.sourceforge.net/sourceforge/secureideas/base-1.1.2.tar.gz

15- Go back to your download directory and run
    cp base-1.1.2.tar.gz /var/www/html/

```
cd /var/www/html
tar –xvzf base-1.1.2.tar.gz
rm –rf base-1.1.2.tar.gz
mv base-1.1.2 base
cd /var/www/html/base/
cp base_conf.php.dist base_conf.php
```

16- Edit the "base_conf.php" file and insert the following perimeters

```
$BASE_urlpath = "/base";
$DBlib_path = "/var/www/adodb/ ";
$DBtype = "mysql";
$alert_dbname = "snort";
$alert_host = "localhost";
$alert_port = "";
$alert_user = "snort";
$alert_password = "password";
/* Archive DB connection parameters */
$archive_exists = 0; # Set this to 1 if you have an archive DB
```

17- You can also configure base more easily by going to http://localhost/base/setup after starting the httpd service.

18- To check if the snort configuration is good, run

```
# snort –c /etc/snort/snort.conf
# /usr/local/bin/snort -c /etc/snort/snort.conf -i eth0 -g snort -D
12- For graphs, you need to install the following pear modules
# pear install Image_Color
# pear install Image_Canvas
# pear install Image_Graph
```

19- To see the list of alerts generated by Snort, just go to http://localhost/base/ after starting the httpd service.

14- Create the startup script:

```
# gedit /etc/init.d/snort-barn
```

Enter the following into the file:

```
#!/bin/bash
/sbin/ifconfig eth0 up
/usr/local/bin/snort -Dq -u snort -g snort -c \
/etc/snort/snort.conf -i eth0
/usr/local/bin/barnyard -c /etc/snort/barnyard.conf -g \
/etc/snort/gen-msg.map -s /etc/snort/sid-msg.map -d \
/var/log/snort -f snort.log -w /etc/snort/bylog.waldo &
```

Make it executable:
#chmod +x /etc/init.d/snort-barn
The command update-rc.d will set up links between files in the directories rc?.d
#update-rc.d snort-barn defaults 95
Reboot and see if it works!

Observation: The program is good for detecting the intrusion in the whole network.

4.3 Installing ACID:

ACID is similar to BAS. It is a graphical interface that assists in monitoring the intrusion alarms in the whole network.

1- Install Snort and configure it in the way shown in the previous section. Create the Snort DB in a similar way.

2- Download ADODB from http://phplens.com/lens/dl/adodb453.tgz and extract it in /var/www/adodb

3- Download Acid from http://acidlab.sourceforge.net/acid-0.9.6b23.tar.gz

4- Download JPGraph and install it.

```
# cd /var/www
# tar -xvzf ~/jpgraph-*.tar.gz
# cd jpgraph-*
# rm -rf README
# rm -rf QPL.txt
5- Install and configure Acid:
# cd /var/www/html
# tar -xvzf ~/acid-0.9.6b23.tar.gz
# cd acid
```

6- Configuring Acid. Edit the acid_conf.php file. It should look like this (except of course you will need your password): The highlighted items are what you need to change

```
$DBlib_path = "/var/www/adodb";
$DBtype = "mysql";
/* Alert DB connection parameters
 * - $alert_dbname : MySQL database name of Snort alert DB
 * - $alert_host : host on which the DB is stored
 * - $alert_port : port on which to access the DB
 * - $alert_user : login to the database with this user
 * - $alert_password : password of the DB user
 *
 * This information can be gleaned from the Snort database
 * output plugin configuration.
 */
$alert_dbname = "snort";
$alert_host = "localhost";
$alert_port = "";
$alert_user = "snort";
$alert_password = "password";
```

```
/* Archive DB connection parameters */
$archive_dbname = "snort";
$archive_host = "localhost";
$archive_port = "";
$archive_user = "snort";
$archive_password = "password ";
And a little further down
$ChartLib_path = "/var/www/jpgraph-1.16/src";
```

7- Go to http://localhost/acid/acid_main.php after restarting snort and httpd service.

Observation: The program is similar to BASE, is good for detecting the intrusion in the whole network.

4.4 Installing Snort Rule Manager rman:

1- Download Snort Rule Manager rman from rman.sourceforge.net and extract it to be a folder /var/www/html/rman

2- Use the mysql.dbschema file to create the additional tables required. The user you login is must have the appropriate create rights on the database
> mysql -p snort < mysql.dbschema

That should have created seven tables in your database prefixed with rman_. Now you need to create a user called rman_www which should have Select Insert Update and Delete rights over the rman_tables created.
> mysql> grant CREATE, INSERT, SELECT, DELETE, UPDATE on snort.* to rman_www @localhost;

3- You need to edit the loadrules.pl script and edit the database configuration. Fill in the database name, user and password and save the file. You then need to execute the script and give the directory where you downloaded the rules as the command line argument:
> #./loadrules.pl /etc/snort/rules

4- The script scans through all files in the rules directory and loads the rules contained in them into a group named after the filename - i.e. the rules in backdoor.rules get added into the group called 'backdoor'. If you want to update the ruleset in the database at any time just download a new ruleset and re-run the command. The script will detect new or modified rules and merge them into the database.

5- Copy rman/configs/db.config and db.timestamp to the snort rules /etc/snort/rules directory.

6- Edit the sensor and database information in the db.config file. Make sure you edit both the double commented lines and the snort config line

7- Edit snort.conf to suit your needs. Add line in bold shown below to snort.conf just below HOME_NET:
> include db.vars
8- Add the following line to the database logging section:
> # database: log to a variety of databases
> include db.config

9- Comment out all the rule includes in the snort.conf file

10- Add an include for the db.rules file to snort.conf:
> # Include all relevant rulesets here

include db.rules

11- Create empty files db.rules, db.vars in /etc/snort/rules
   # touch db.rules
   # touch db.vars

12- Edit the /var/www/html/rman/rman_common.inc file and fill in the $dbuser, $dbpass fields just after the copyright notice

13- Start the httpd service

14 Start the rman by going to http://localhost/rman. If you select sensor maintenance, and then click the 'Add Sensor' button you should see your new sensors listed. Select the sensors you want to activate and click the activate button. The page should now redisplay minus the sensor you just activated. Select the 'Return to Sensor Maintenance' link at the top and you should now see you sensor listed there. Select your sensor and start assigning groups etc.

Observation: I see the program is good in seeing the snort rules and preprocessors and variables, but I did not see options for adding new rules.

4.5 Installing SnortCenter:

1- Download and install the SnortCenter console. You can find it at http://users.pandora.be/larc/download/.

```
# tar -zxvf SnortCenter-1.0-RC1
# cd www
# mkdir /var/www/html/snortcenter
# cp –R * /var/www/html/snortcenter
# cd /var/www/html/snortcenter
# gedit config.php
Edit the following lines in config.php.
$DBlib_path = "/var/www/adodb"
$DB_user = "root"
$DB_password=""
$hidden_key_num = "123456"
```

2- Now we need to create the SnortCenter database:

```
# mysql –u root –p
mysql> CREATE DATABASE snortcenter;
mysql> exit
```

You can access the SnortCenter console at http://localhost/snortcenter. The default account is "admin" with the password "change".

3- For SnortCenter agent installation, install dependencies for using SSL connections with SnortCenter. You can download Net_SSLeay from http://symlabs.com/Net_SSLeay/.

```
# cp Net_SSLeayrpm-*-**.tar.gz /usr/src/redhat/SOURCES
# cd /usr/src/redhat/SOURCES
# tar –zxvf  Net_SSLeay.pm
# cd Net_*
# perl Makefile.PL
# make install
```

4- Start the Snortcenter agent install.

```
# mkdir /opt/snortagent/
# cp snortcenter-agent-v0.1.6*.tar.gz /opt/snortagent
# cd /opt/snortagent
# tar -zxvf snortcenter-agent-v0.1.6*.tar.gz
# cd sensor
# ./setup.sh
```

5- You will then be prompted with a series of questions:

```
Config File Directory = /etc/snort
Log File Directory = /var/log/snort
```

```
Perl = <ENTER>
Snort = <ENTER>
Snort Rule Config File = /etc/snort
Port = <ENTER>
IP Address = (Your sensors management IP (eth0) )
Login Name = admin
Password = (Password that the consoles uses to access the sensor)
Confirm Password = (Same as above)
Host = <ENTER>
SSL = Y
Allow IP = (This is the IP address of you SnortCenter Server)
Start on Boot = Y
```

6- You can go to the console that users can use to access the sensor by browsing http://localhost:2525

4- Once you have the SnortCenter agent installed you need to tell the SnortCenter console about it. Access the SnortCenter website http://localhost/snortcente you setup and add a new sensor. Click save and go to sensor view.Now we need to push our defaults rules and settings to the sensor. Click on PUSH. Then you can start using the SnortCenter

Observation: I see the program has a good capabilities to manage and configure snort. But it did not work very well with me. It did not even push the snort configuration. I will leave it for your trial.

4.6 OSSEC:

OSSEC HIDS is an Open Source Host-based Intrusion Detection System. It performs log analysis, integrity checking, rootkit detection, time-based alerting and active response. If you have one system to monitor, you can install the OSSEC HIDS locally on that box and do everything from there. However, if you are administering a few systems, you can select one to be your OSSEC server and the others to be OSSEC agents, forwarding events to the server for analysis.

1-Download the latest version http://www.ossec.net/files/ossec-hids-latest.tar.gz.

2- Extract the compressed package and run the "./install.sh" script (It will guide you through the installation).
```
# tar -zxvf ossec-hids-*.tar.gz (or gunzip -d; tar -xvf)
# cd ossec-hids-*
# ./install.sh
```

3- Start the OSSEC HIDS.
```
# /var/ossec/bin/ossec-control start
```

4- Configuration options:
The OSSEC HIDS configuration is mostly done inside the ossec.conf file (by default at /var/ossec/etc/ossec.conf). This file must always start with the root element of ossec_config, followed by one of the following configuration sections:

> Global: default options everywhere in the system.
> Rules: list of rules to be included.
> Syscheck: configuration related to the syscheck - integrity check.
> Rootcheck: Configuration related to the rootcheck - rootkit detection.
> Alerts; email and log alerting options.
> Localfile: options related to the log files to be monitored.
> Remote: configuration related to remote connections.
> Client: agent related options.
> Command: active-response configuration.
> Active response: Active response configuration.

5- Some of these options should only be used by the "agent" installation and some should only be used on the "server" or "local" installations. The list bellow shows each installation type and their options:
server: global, rules, syscheck, rootcheck, alerts, localfile, remote, command and active-response.
local: global, rules, syscheck, rootcheck, alerts, localfile, command and active-response.

You can go to www.ossec.net for understandong the configuration options.

6- The communication between the server and the agents is secure (encrypted and authenticated). Because of that, for every "agent" that you want to install, you need to create an "authentication key" for it on the server. When the key is generated on the server, you need export it from there an import on the agent. First, you need to add the agent to the server. You just need to run the "manage_agents" command, provide the IP Address of the agent and choose a name for it (or username).
/var/ossec/bin/manage_agents

4.7. Sguil:

Sguil (pronounced sgweel) is built by network security analysts for network security analysts. Sguil's main component is an intuitive GUI that provides access to realtime events, session data, and raw packet captures. Sguil facilitates the practice of Network Security Monitoring and event driven analysis. The Sguil client is written in tcl/tk and can be run on any operating system that supports tcl/tk (including Linux, *BSD, Solaris, MacOS, and Win32). Sguil should be installed in the following order:
    Step 1: Install mysql and create the sguil database.
    Step 2: Install the GUI server (sguild).
    Step 3: Install the GUI client (sguil.tk).
    Step 4: Install the sensor.

Sguil seems to be good package. I tried installing Sguil and I succeeded in installing the Server and Client, but I got problem in installing the sensor. For installing the sensor, you should install the Snort and Barnyard package, and I got an error when I started the Barnyard. Also patching the Snort and Barnyard for Sguil use ends with error. So I just will leave that for your trial.

5. Conclusion:

In this paper I evaluated some the security tools. The paper covered the installation and configuration of the following security tools: LANguard, Nessus, Snort, BASE, ACID, Rman, SnorCenter, OSSEC, Sguil.

6. References:

[1] http://www.snort.org web site.
[2] http://sectools.org/ web site.
[3] http://www.nessus.org/
[4] http://www.gfi.com/lannetscan/
[5] http://www.ossec.net/
[6] http://sguil.sourceforge.net/
[7] http://rman.sourceforge.net/